# ELSEWHERE: AN ELEGY

# Elsewhere

## AN ELEGY

## FAISAL
## MOHYUDDIN

Published by
Next Page Press
San Antonio, Texas
www.nextpage-press.com
© 2024 Faisal Mohyuddin. All rights reserved.

ISBN: 978-1-7366721-5-0
Library of Congress Control Number: 2023948967

*Book team:*
Laura Van Prooyen, Director and Editor
Amber Morena, Book Design

Cover Painting: *My Father's Songs* by Faisal Mohyuddin

*for Zayan*

Maybe closure is the first loss, the first order of business, is sealed until its time has come, and, when the time never comes, is the one thing, in never arriving, that remains just as we need it.

—MATTHEW KELSEY

He would say
the world is full of secrets.
He would say
listen.

—SHAM-E-ALI NAYEEM

# Contents

**V.**

# LAMPLIGHT

When it arrives,
when its time

to arrive arrives
much too soon,

grief casts
the longest,

most private
shadows, then

buries them
beneath its

endless arriving,
the luminous

splendor
of the before-

life still there,
held in sky-

lark nests,
each a mercy

from which
some passage

into solace
might hatch.

Let me believe
as this steadfast

tenderness
believes,

in being able
to unlatch

every ache,
translate

absence into
longing,

longing into
bird, flight

into prayer,
prayer into

key, key
into more

grains of sand,
and this ever-

gathering
weight of loss

into lamp-
light, river-

song—a son
barbed with

questions,
impatience,

the illusion
of abundance,

oblivious
to his grieving

father's
unstillness,

his ancestral
terror.

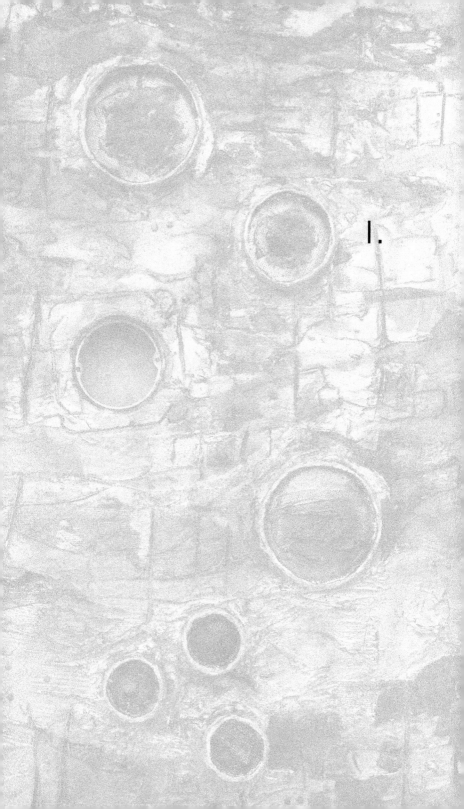

I.

I skip ahead
to the end of the story
and find God

has given refuge
in the body

of a bird.

# The River. The Beckoning. The Chandeliers.

*A haibun for the elders, their ghosts*

In some rooms, the outstretched hands of past selves begging for another chance. In others, your childhood face, smudged with mango ice cream, smiling. At the top of the staircase, a box taped shut, your twinkling share of night folded up and stored within, a blanket for your most difficult days. Down the hall, a tiny river, a toy boat drifting toward music. If there is a kitchen, heaven is there, or a door that opens into heaven. And an hourglass balanced on the threshold. Close your eyes now, let your hands guide you along the walls until you stand at the front door. Unfasten its many latches, open your eyes, feast on the sweet animal taste of your own voice, its beauty, its might. Delight in the newness that comes with growing old. Savor the piercing scent of cloves, their dusty fire, the fearlessness of the dying. Cross over, cross back.

Inside again, your face hardens. Your elders, who like chandeliers have been studying you from above, recognize the beckoning in the winds blowing in, whispering, *No, not yet.*

So you return to the riverbank, stumble back into the arms of ghosts.

Once, you were born and did not survive.

Once, you grew old and died.

Once, you lived, outlived, had many rooms to explore,
could blueprint new ones when your rummaging
left you wanting, when the bulbs burned so intensely,
they needed more hours to pour their radiance into.

10

Months of rain followed, months of rain and rising panic. Then this prayer, this crumbling edifice.

Moored now inside it, a confession:


Your tongue another
    boat, its body a needle,
        the river its thread.

# An End to Captivity

*If*

*I go walking through*

    *dawn's dewy shadows*

*toward the river*

    *where the carp burst through*

*the gleaming muck*

    *to belch air, and there,*

*in the echoes*

    *I catch the wordless*

*voice of my dead*

    *father—*

        *then*

    *should the unexpected gift*

*of my child's embraces*

    *awaiting my return*

*be like a key?*

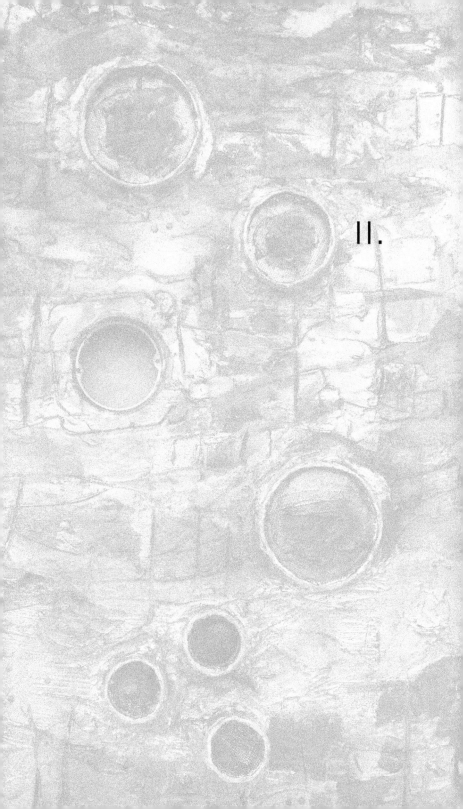

II.

Outside my room,
a steady rain,
its voice

                              primitive, desolate,
                              consoling—

          my father's.

# The Jar. The Mist. The Bewilderment.

*A haibun for the ones who listen*

Today, more troubles and the trickery of the mind. The air ghosting through the cemetery still laden with the murk of old glass, like that of the jar I am holding. A scoop of wet earth within. The paths cutting through the tombs teeming with worms, behind them trails of churned mud. A calligraphy spelling out more tales of estrangement.

Before I learned squeamishness, when I was too sheltered to know another's pain, my father taught me how to pierce a worm's saddle with a fishhook, to flex my thumb back as I curled the barbed tip through the flesh to keep from drawing my own blood. I couldn't always make out the words, couldn't sort them from the thumping in his chest, nor tolerate the throttling blows of everyday noise. Hyperacusis is a curse. Sound becomes another's accidental weapon, why so often I am climbing into myself, shrinking away from suffering. Grief, too, demands we turn inward.

> Yet through this misty quiet, I can hear my father's voice, the lure of it, the way it still beckons me toward water, toward a lighter torment.

I pluck from the pavement a few worms, drop them in the jar, watch mesmerized as they wriggle back into darkness, convinced they are safe, in God's care, immortal. I don't remember when I fell from the nest of my parents' dreams, but ever since, I can't stop trying to translate their miseries into this kind of holiness.

> Perhaps every shelter is housed within a larger house of terror housed within the larger house of mercy.

Perhaps every saint is a failed child seeking forgiveness, every uncaught fish another reason to think miracles rely on bewilderment and dumb luck.

Soon, the sun will cleave open the clouds, hush for a spell the rumors of more rain, the bombardments of thunder. The jar I set sideways on the ground signifies the heft the living carry in a place such as this.

My ears, crippled. Sound
    pierces, ruptures—distances
        me from God's mercy.

# An End to Captivity

*What lies buried beneath*

    *this wreckage of loss? The solace*

*of my father's songs, another lost*

    *geography never meant for me.*

*Quietly, I ease my son back*

    *into bed, promise him a toy truck,*

*a rocket ride to an imagined*

    *country in some unexplored*

*corner of the galaxy—whatever he wants*

    *in this age of unlimited*

*wonder, if he would just fold himself*

    *back into a warm pocket of sleep.*

*Next to him, I sit, listening*

    *backwards through his soft*

*wheezing, wondering at the hours*

    *my father spent like this, my body*

*beside his a collection of hungers,*

    *his own father's body reduced*

*to riddles—the light of day*

    *the only thing that loosened*

*the strangle of longing*

    *by granting him*

*another chance*

    *not to grieve,*

*but to give.*

III.

When a dream
returns him
to me, my father

                                        hands me
                                        a nest

            filled with water.

# The Well. The Dagger.
# The Ones Who Never Arrived.

*A haibun for the forgotten*

If the fish in my bones, salmoning against the rush of blood, could speak about banditry, then what treachery would they sing about to sing light into these crumbling tunnels? If every traveler could exhume the countless crimes they carry within their bodies, then might tragedy become less terrifying? If you take the word of the doctors who tried to save him, it was cardiac arrest that took my father's life.

But doesn't the story of every death begin inside a well, well before birth, within the tangled mysteries of a more troubled time?

> And wasn't what really killed him
> a heart that had been broken? Too many times
> to weather another shock? To survive

> as long as he did—
> that should remain
> the greater miracle.

He was a child of Partition, a toddler born into an already broken world who climbed out a well and learned to straggle his way beyond the bloodshed lurking forever between one silence and the next. On what grounds could anyone demand more breath for a migrant like him? Who instead would have had to die first? Think of grief then as a gift, its disorienting weight a blessing.

> Wonder, blindness,
> those flashes of doubt,

of asking why
God keeps such distances—

all are possible
because of theft, massacre,

fortune and misfortune,
the mythologies of innocence.

\* \* \*

Generations ago, between one doom and another, there loomed the prospect for survival, and someone desperate enough to steal must have daggered out from a fellow refugee's grasp a safe passage for their own bloodline. Without their crimes, try to imagine your entire tree felled. Try to imagine oblivion. Do not imagine the swift plunge of the blade, the blood of it still mooned under your fingernails.

Who is that ancestor
you betray now
with your stupid worries?

You're still young,
young enough to listen,
to unlock the door,
to greet God with a body
ready to receive mercy.

If history ever finds you, sitting alone on the cracked floor of this lightless room, listening to the thunder of distant explosions, will you stash your shame beneath the floorboards before surrendering to combat?

Or will you too have your curse-choked throat slit by an unwanted guest, the carcass of your failings tossed into a river where it will transform

into a fish

hellbent on being

snagged back out

into the suffocating air,

dying of desire,

hooked by a hunger

to forget?

* * *

Swim with me, child—free
me from the endless swindlings
of reinvention.

# An End to Captivity

*Every day the child asks*

*the same question:*

When

will I be

older too?

*The answer: a rising flood*

*of worries, without a tongue to taste*

*the perfect quiet, to protest*

*the loneliness, to barter with God,*

*to implore Him to trade this*

*half-lit exile looming in the wake of loss*

*for the fragrance of the last*

*remaining blossom of that long-ago-*

*abandoned tree I imagine*

*my grandfather planted to mark*

*my father's birth, to bless his future*

*with an abundance of dutiful children*

*and an exaltation of songbirds*

*to forever keep the living afloat.*

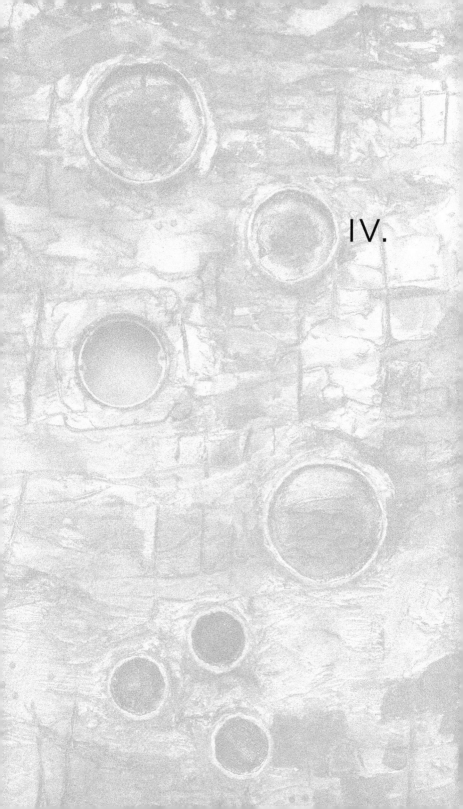

IV.

The boy who
planted the tree
once swam

in lullaby, then
climbed out a father,

estranged.

# The Stoic. The Playground.
# The Raw Material of Myth-Making.

*A haibun for the cowards*

Let me this evening accompany the falling shadows, solace my mind with the silly banter of the playgrounds my father and I built between us, our unspoken way of ensuring the earth did not split open our silences.

> The unlived hours of his life have become the raw material of my myth-making, just as his father's truncated life became the source of his own private music—how he came to understand that sometimes the best remedy for sorrow is separation.

When he was only a child, in the wake of his father's death, and again when tragedy stole his first love who he'd met in his third homeland, my father recognized nothing in life is promised, that to fashion an existence built too heavily upon caution is to believe your life matters more than that of others.

> A curse, to be so selfless.

No matter how much I try, I can't emulate his stoicism in the face of suffering, nor remain so rooted in frailty that I squander countless nights of rest praying for impossible outcomes: the absence of strife, forgiveness that heals, the immortality of others. Loss teaches us to know loss, but learning its lessons too well can unearth stranger worries, anguishes disguised as fidelity, even the kind of love that fish-hooks the heart and wrenches it out through the mouth.

> Do you see why I crave the companionship of an imagined father, prefer to pretend I am a child untouched by despair?

But from what wellspring of loss do these songs come?

Into whose life do they gather now, each as nectar,
as balm, as answer?

Father, if you can hear me as I can hear you, then offer a word of
comfort. If it is my fate to become a well in your absence, then teach
me how to find in its depths enough bucketfuls of water to cleanse
the cowardice from my conscience.


God taught us panic,
its simple logic a lamp
guiding us back home.

# An End to Captivity

*Within, a door, locked.*

*Behind it, the innocence*

*of a skylark, waiting*

*to be slaughtered.*

*My son knows nothing yet*

*of this nightly searching*

*for songs. Secrets*

*do not torment his wonders*

*yet. To devour*

*the bird's wings is to taste*

*the night sky in summer,*

*to commune with the bleakness*

*of every breathing body,*

*to kneel without complaint*

*before the wintering*

*touch of a child's eagerness*

*to become older,*

    *their impossible wish*

*for deathless tomorrows.*

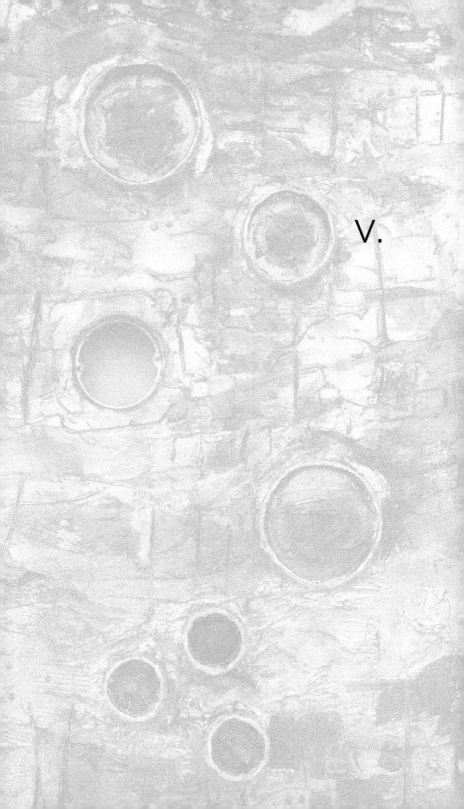

V.

You catch your breath
these days
by seeking God

                                        but forget sometimes
                                        to merely




                    listen.

# The Hourglass. The Pebble.
# The Throne of God.

*A haibun for the fatherless*

Inside the lightless language of elegy, where each day the waking musk of roses makes more strange the semantics of loss, I could choose the path of forgetting, temple the embering tenderness between brackets, and become less hunched by hunger than I am. Or simply embrace the terror.

> If transcendence is still possible in a world as battered-down as this one, then maybe it's better I let the listening dawn ladder my now-kindled tongue back down to God. There, kneeling at His throne, I could say to Him, I am sorry for my weaknesses, for every strange wish held meekly in my anguish.

> > I could even relinquish my delirium
> > for a more immediate doom,
> > rush to wade through low tides of sunlight
> > until the landscape hastens
> > toward surrender.

I could, with a scoop of glistening earth, entomb my better ear, the one less ravaged by hyperacusis, then toss from its mantle the hourglass, listen to its shattering botch my mumbled prayers. All this despite the heaps of mud meant to quiet the upheaval. Or, as the distance between us will always be forever, I could loosen the trembling clutch of longing by pronouncing the pebble of your name, over and over as if performing zikr, until it comes to sound more like sand, until it too can sift more serenely through the songless hours of this fatherless life. O Father, please forgive me.

I've still not divined
    how to unhusk this steadfast
        grief from my poems.

# An End to Captivity

*An invented memory—*

> *Your father on the other side*
>
> *of the hourglass, gazing*
>
> *into your newborn eyes,*
>
> *discovering within*
>
> *their wild brightness*
>
> *the first verses of devotion.*

*And you, held*

> *in your mother's arms,*
>
> *wincing as that first burst of light*
>
> *severs body from body,*
>
> *as rivers of breath*
>
> *pour freely from your tiny lungs.*

*And Paradise?*

> *Beneath a mother's feet.*
>
> *For fathers, a myth and a mirror.*

*A stopping place for grief.*

*An elsewhere for the helpless.*

*Where your child goes*

>   *to find you*

>   *when you have left*

>   *them behind*

>   *in a world overrun*

>   *by absences.*

# RIVERSONG

Convinced
I can breathe

under water,
I plunge

into this ever-
arriving river

of shadows,
summoned

by a needling
glint of steel,

a new promise
of rescue,

one ferried
not through

the torment
of longing,

but carried
with love upon

the turbulent
thrum of

birdwings
thrashing

against
the living

surface
of devotion.

From just
beneath

its mad rush,
I reach up

through
the bubbly

murk, grab
my son's

steadying hand,
ready to be

fished out by
his innocence—

but what if
I decide

instead
to pull him

into
the under-

tow too, to
introduce him

to the hazards
of passing

time, to save
him from

becoming
another shelter-

craving child
consumed

by this
forever-

long search
for the healing

language
of stillness,

the quiet
mercy

of else-
where?

# Acknowledgments

Many thanks to the editors of these journals where the following poems first appeared, sometimes in different forms:

*The Aleph Review:* "Five Answers to the Same Question"
*The Banyan Review:* "Lamplight"
*Chicago Quarterly Review:* "The End to Captivity"
*Pleiades:* "The Well. The Dagger. The Ones Who Never Arrived."
*Poet Lore:* "The River. The Beckoning. The Chandeliers."

Lines from Matthew Kelsey's poem "Memorial, Virtually Speaking" (*American Poetry Review*, 51.3) are used as an epigraph with permission of the author.

Lines from Sham-e-Ali Nayeem's poem "Invocation" (*City of Pearls*, Upset Press, 2019) are used as an epigraph with permission of the author.

Thank you to the many people who have offered encouragement and guidance and input along the way: Zafar Malik, Atamjit Singh, Neela Banerjee, Dante Di Stefano, Tarfia Faizullah, Adeeba Shahid Talukder, Shadab Zeest Hashmi, Afshan Shafi, Rajiv Mohabir, Taz Ahmed, Seema Reza, k. eltinaé, Sahar Muradi, Dilruba Ahmed, Mary Barbara Moore, KC Trommer, Tara Skurtu, Zeina Hashem Beck, Sam Herschel Wein, George Abraham, Mariam Gomaa, Ramy El-Etreby, Naoko Fujimoto, Sadia Uqaili, Kazim Ali, Stephen Byrne, Pádraig Ó Tuama, Greg Hewett, Aaron Coleman, Amy Danzer, Christine Sneed, John O'Connor, Jack

Ridl, Ignatius Valentine Aloysius, Rebecca Morgan Frank, Daniel Borzutzky, Raymond Antrobus, Li-Young Lee, Clare Rossini, Rosebud Ben-Oni, Randy Albers, Donald E. Evans, Syed Afzal Haider, Dipika Mukherjee, Virginia Bell, Rebecca Gayle Howell, Sachin Patel, Ariel and Melissa Tesher, Shervon Cassim, Alfonso Li, Jeremy Thimm, Samantha Kennedy, Beth Prusiecki, Paul Lusson, Danielle Speciale, Julia Kapelnikova, Blake Novotny, Paul Swanson, Stephanie Solis, Rachel Alongi, Beth Ahlgrim, Crystal Simone Smith, Tony Fitzpatrick, Su Hwang, Sung Yun Shin, Said Shaiye, Chris Aldana, Czaerra Galicinao Ucol, Samina Hadi-Tabassum, Shireen and Afzal Ahmed, Syed Atif Rizwan, Mishika Narula, Sanah Ahsan, and Arica Hilton. In loving memory of Miguel Cervantes and Rizwan Kadir.

Thank you to my Poet's Table Chicago crew: Matthew Kelsey, Lindsay Garbutt, Ann Hudson, Casey Thayer, Jacob Saenz, Willie James, Tara Ebrahimi, and Cate Lycurgus. Thank you to my colleagues and students at Highland Park High School (particularly everyone in the English Department) and at the School of Professional Studies at Northwestern University. Thank you to Narrative 4, especially Lisa Consiglio, Colum McCann, Lee Keylock, Karen Hollins, Kandice Cole, Darrell Bourque, Felice Belle, Charles Miles, and Greg Khalil who often shares the wisdom of Reverend Mitri Raheb of Bethlehem, Palestine: that *hope* must be understood and practiced *as a verb*. Thank you to all my teachers, professors, and mentors.

For their generous and thoughtful blurbs, and for their beautiful poems, huge admiration-filled thanks to Ashley M. Jones and Greg Santos. For allowing me to use lines from their incredible poems as epigraphs, and for their friendship and wisdom, thank you to Matthew Kelsey and to Sham-e-Ali Nayeem.

To my new family at Next Page Press—I am beyond thrilled to receive such a warm welcome from you all. Thank you, Amber Morena, for your lovely cover and book design. And to Laura Van Prooyen: a boundless shout of gratitude. I can only begin to express just how joyful and affirming it has been to work with you on *Elsewhere: An Elegy*. Thank you for ushering this book into the world, and for doing so with such care, patience, and insight.

A very special thank you to the following friends whose guidance was essential in the writing and rewriting of this book: Hari Alluri, Leah Umansky, Juan Pablo Mobili, and Kevin Lakani.

To my family—the Mohyuddins and the Sodhas, and all my aunts, uncles, cousins, and relatives—thank you for all the love, faith, and affirmation. The grief that sits at the heart of these poems is a shared grief, and a product of the love we all had for my late father and late father-in-law. May both men rest in peace and light. Ameen. Endless love and reverence to my mother Rahat and my mother-in-law Hawa; despite their grief, they remain as strong, giving, and vibrant as they can be.

To dearest Hina and Zayan, endless love and gratitude for making this life possible.

Alhamdulillah.

The final edits to this manuscript were made in October and November of 2023, at a time when thousands of innocent people were being killed indiscriminately. I couldn't then—and still can't now—stop imagining the unfathomable and crushing weight of the grief. The individual grief. The collective grief. The grief children will carry for the rest of their lives, that people will be buried with, that will be inherited by coming generations. The grief that gives shape to future anguish, and that remains a part of the lands upon which we live, anywhere and everywhere. Grief's reach is always wider and deeper than we recognize. May God grant patience, fortitude, comfort, voice, and hope for all those in mourning then, now, and hereafter. May this grief become a catalyst for seeing and speaking truth, ensuring freedom and safety, promoting justice and healing, and establishing a lasting peace—for *all*, always. Ameen.

# About the Author

Faisal Mohyuddin is the author of *The Displaced Children of Displaced Children* (Eyewear Publishing, 2018) and *The Riddle of Longing* (Backbone Press, 2017). He teaches English at Highland Park High School in suburban Chicago and creative writing at Northwestern University's School  of Professional Studies. He also serves as a Master Practitioner with the global not-for-profit Narrative 4 and is a visual artist. *www.faisalmohyuddin.com*

Printed in the USA
CPSIA information can be obtained
at www.ICGtesting.com
JSHW020543270224
57928JS00003B/124